DRAGONFLIES

INSECTS

James P. Rowan

The Rourke Corporation, Inc.
Vero Beach, Florida 32964

Edited by Sandra A. Robinson

PHOTO CREDITS
© Lynn M. Stone: cover, title page, pages 4, 7, 8, 10, 13, 15, 21;
© Jerry Hennen: pages 12, 18; © James P. Rowan: page 17

Library of Congress Cataloging-in-Publication Data

Rowan, James P.
    Dragonflies / by James P. Rowan.
        p. cm. — (The Insect discovery library)
    Includes index.
    Summary: An introduction to the physical characteristics, habits,
and behavior of dragonflies.
    ISBN 0-86593-287-5
    1. Dragonflies—Juvenile literature. [1. Dragonflies.]
I. Title. II. Series.
QL520.R69 1993
595.7'33—dc20   89-32926
                                                       CIP
Printed in the USA   AC

TABLE OF CONTENTS

DRAGONFLIES

Dragonflies are large, colorful insects that live "two lives." They live the "first life" under water. They live the "second life" as creatures of land and air.

Dragonflies can fly quickly from one place to another. They can also **hover** in the air, like helicopters.

A dragonfly's two large eyes bulge from its head. They can look in every direction for **prey,** the little animals that dragonflies eat.

Dragonflies are flying jewels of meadows and marshes

HOW DRAGONFLIES LOOK

Dragonflies have pencil-shaped bodies with two pairs of large wings that look like a hair bow. The wings have many wirelike **veins.** In fact, dragonfly wings look much like **transparent,** or clear, leaves because of the veins.

Dragonflies come in many different colors, depending upon the kind, or **species,** of dragonfly. Some are fire engine red. Others are bright blue and green.

Clear, veined wings of many dragonflies and damselflies look like cellophane paper

KINDS OF DRAGONFLIES

Over 5,000 species of dragonflies live on Earth. Over 450 kinds live in the United States.

The green darner is a common species. It is about 2 1/2 inches long with a 6-inch wingspread. That is not wide compared to an eagle's wingspread, but it makes a large insect.

Another common dragonfly, the ten-spot, was named for the dark spots on its wings.

A ten-spot dragonfly, alert for prey, lands on a favorite perch

DAMSELFLIES

Damselflies are the slender relatives of dragonflies. Damselflies usually hold their four wings close to their bodies when resting. Dragonflies hold their wings outstretched, like airplane wings.

Like their larger cousins, damselflies begin life under water and feed on young mosquitoes. Adult damselflies, like dragonflies, are **predators**— hunting animals. They often catch flying mosquitoes.

11

Another jewel of the meadow, the slender damselfly

An adult dragonfly emerges from its nymph skin

A damselfly deposits her eggs under marsh plants

WHERE DRAGONFLIES LIVE

Adult dragonflies live near water or in open, grassy areas. They often have a favorite resting spot, such as a branch or rock, where they watch for prey. Even if it is scared away, a dragonfly will usually return to the same perch.

Dragonflies like to hunt on warm, sunny days. At night and on cloudy days, they usually rest. They hide in grass and shrubs.

A dragonfly perches on a glasswort stem near a saltwater bay

FROM EGG TO ADULT

Female dragonflies lay eggs in ponds, marshes and swamps. The young dragonfly that hatches from an egg is called a **nymph.** It does not look very much like its parents. The nymph lives under water and hunts for food among **aquatic plants,** or water-loving plants.

A dragonfly stays a nymph for as long as two years. As it grows, it sheds its skin several times. After one final shed, the nymph flies away as an adult dragonfly.

*Dragonfly nymphs hunt
in tiny jungles of aquatic plants*

INDEX

Glossary

aquatic (uh KWAT ihk) — living in water

hover (HO ver) — to hang fluttering in the air

nymph (NIMPF) — a stage in the life of a young insect; the young of certain insects

predator (PRED uh tor) — an animal that kills other animals for food

prey (PRAY) — an animal that is hunted for food by another animal

species (SPEE sheez) — within a group of closely-related animals, such as dragonflies, one certain kind or type (*ten-spot* dragonfly)

tadpole (TAD pole) — the fishlike stage of baby frogs and toads when they live in water

transparent (tranz PARE ent) — clear

vein (VAYN) — a wirelike structure that strengthens the wings of insects

DRAGONFLIES AND PEOPLE

Most people like dragonflies and damselflies. These insects kill mosquitoes, and they are fun to watch as they buzz the quiet surface of a pond.

A few people, however, foolishly fear dragonflies and damselflies because they are sometimes called "stingers" or "sewing needles."

Dragonflies and damselflies are harmless to people. They do not bite, sting or make needle marks. Enjoy them!

DRAGONFLY ENEMIES

Sometimes the hunter becomes the hunted. That is certainly true with dragonflies.

Dragonfly nymphs are food for fish, frogs and other aquatic animals, including the diving beetles known as water tigers.

Adult dragonflies are snatched in mid-air by such fast-flying birds as flycatchers and martins. Sometimes dragonflies are trapped in spider webs.

Trapped! A damselfly is prey to a banded argiope spider

WHAT DRAGONFLIES EAT

Dragonflies are fierce hunters as both nymphs and adults. Nymphs eat small insects, small fish, and baby frogs and toads, or **tadpoles.**

Adult dragonflies hunt flying insects, especially mosquitoes and gnats. Dragonflies use their six legs like a basket and catch prey in mid-air. They usually eat while they are flying.

On cool nights, droplets of dew collect on dragonfly wings. Dragonflies must wait for the sun to dry their wings and warm their bodies before they begin to hunt.

Successful hunt—a dragonfly clutches its butterfly prey

MEM FOX

Tough Boris

Illustrated by

KATHRYN BROWN

Voyager Books
Harcourt Brace & Company
San Diego   New York   London

With special thanks to Allyn Johnston, Janet Green,
Joe, Paul, BZ, and Eric
—K.B.

First Voyager Books edition 1998
Voyager Books is a registered trademark of Harcourt Brace & Company.

The Library of Congress has cataloged the hardcover edition as follows:
Fox, Mem, 1946–
Tough Boris/Mem Fox; illustrated by Kathryn Brown.—1st ed.
p. cm.
Summary: Boris von der Borch is a tough pirate, but he cries when his
parrot dies.
ISBN 0-15-289612-0
ISBN 0-15-201891-3 pb
[1. Pirates—Fiction.] I. Brown, Kathryn, 1955– ill. II. Title.
PZ7.F8373To 1994
[E]—dc20 92-8015

E F D

Printed in Singapore

The illustrations in this book were done in watercolor on Waterford paper.
The display and text type were set in Cochin by Harcourt Brace & Company
Photocomposition Center, San Diego, California.
Color separations by Bright Arts, Ltd., Singapore
Printed and bound by Tien Wah Press, Singapore
This book was printed on Arctic matte paper.
Production supervision by Stanley Redfern and Jane Van Gelder
Designed by Camilla Filancia

For Alexia and Helen
and, of course,
Paul von der Borch
—M. F.

For Parker, Sawyer, Will,
Levi, and Amos
—K. B.

Once upon a time, there lived a
pirate named Boris von der Borch.

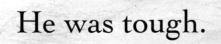

He was tough.

All pirates are tough.

He was massive.
All pirates are massive.

He was scruffy.

All pirates are scruffy.

He was greedy.

All pirates are greedy.

He was fearless.

All pirates
are fearless.

He was scary.

All pirates are scary.

But when his parrot died,

he cried and cried.

All pirates cry.

And so do I.